EDGE

✳

EDGE

❋

MARCIA ALDRICH

NEW MICHIGAN PRESS

TUCSON, ARIZONA

NEW MICHIGAN PRESS

DEPT OF ENGLISH, P. O. BOX 210067

UNIVERSITY OF ARIZONA

TUCSON, AZ 85721-0067

<http://newmichiganpress.com>

Orders and queries to <nmp@thediagram.com>.

ISBN 978-1-934832-83-7. FIRST PRINTING.

Design by Ander Monson.

Cover Photo 138797168 © Chumphon Whangchom
| Dreamstime.com.

CONTENTS

A CHAIR INHABITS A DREAM

The chair is built of oak with a dark stain. Picture it in a one room school house set in a clearing. Small and old-fashioned, one size fits all. Sturdy in its square design, unlikely to tip over in a scramble, the desk top blossoms from the right arm, and can't be lifted or lowered at will. One position for the desk, but also for those sitting in it. The wood is scarred with names and stars.

❅

The first I remember was in Miss Joy's first grade class room. She used to command the class to be silent. *Silence*, she'd say, demanding it, ruling it to be so. Imposing it. Breaking us to attain it.

One day my mother sent me to school outfitted in a fancy white dress and told me I'd better come home with the dress in the same condition. But at recess I couldn't bear to stay away from the play equipment. I climbed the monkey bars and hung upside down. The sheeny white dress flew over my face, and Bruce Wray, who was always hanging around me unwanted, taunted me with "I can see your underpants, I can see your underpants."

I jumped down from the bars and punched Bruce Wray in the stomach. A crowd quickly gathered, and in the skirmish that ensued, I tore the white dress. Miss Joy materialized and ordered me to get up out of the dust and march straight to the principal's office whereupon my mother was called.

❊

Hanging upside down on the monkey bars in a dress, punching boys—these were not the pleasing comportment my mother expected. While we were waiting for my mother to arrive, Miss Joy roped me to the chair, and put tape across my mouth. When my mother made her way to the classroom and saw me strapped to the chair, my mouth covered, she did not gasp in disbelief or disapproval. She smiled at Miss Joy and said, "Yes, that's the appropriate response."

❊

Deborah returned to our sixth-grade homeroom at Jefferson Elementary with white bandages wrapped about her wrists. No one knew why she had tried to kill herself, just that she had. We observed her chosen technique, or at least the locale of her incision. We didn't talk about it. We talked about how Joe lived with his ten brothers and sisters in a one room house without running water, how Victoria's mother packed a moldy sandwich with a wilted lip of lettuce in her lunch box. We sought out every child's vulnerability and taunted them, but when Deborah's mother sent her back to school with her wrists freshly wounded, we didn't say a word, not to Deborah and not among ourselves. She sat in her chair, a chair just like the one I had been strapped to, as if she was made of stone. If Deborah, the most beautiful and successful among us, wanted to stop living, what was in store for us? Why had her mother sent her back to school before the wounds healed to sit in that chair?

My chair was right behind Deborah's. One day in sixth hour geography I cut a snippet of her dark hair. It curled around my finger as if it belonged there.

✻

Near the oaks at the bottom of the dream, cows down in the tall pale grass. Sitting in a wooden chair blunt and small, a chair from grade school, a woman. Dressed in a long-sleeved black gown with a plastic vinyl veil that blots her face. A great bouquet of red roses has spilled its juice onto her lap. The black veil is a blindfold. The cows are arranged in a circle around the woman in the chair, blocking all access to her. They are devouring the long grass before her. I am walking down the hill as I have every day of my dream, walking towards her, when she rips the plastic veil from her face. Mother.

✻

At the eternal birthday party the chairs are arranged in rows like pews. When the music starts, children decked out in their Sunday best, push and shove to reach an empty chair before the music stops. *Safe*, they think, except for one. Then the music begins again.

❀

In the pasture of the dead, two horses, a palomino and a rhone, graze in the late sun. Sitting in the tall grass a chair with an apple on its seat. Waxy red and perfect. The horses will not take the offering.

❀

If I close my eyes, I can see it in the ribbon house of my soul, the chair, my feet dangling over its bars.

EDGE

In every man's heart there is a secret nerve that answers to the vibration of beauty.

—Christopher Morley

Start with a dead deer at the side of Hamilton Road. A major artery between Okemos and Dobie roads, it is my route to work, to the supermarket, to the post office and bank, and the only means of access to Tacoma Hills, the subdivision in Meridian Township where I have lived for the last five years. The speed limit on Hamilton is 25 miles per hour, slowing to 15 at the roundabout a quarter mile to the west. Nevertheless, a driver has struck the deer, and now it lies in the grass in front of a condominium complex. It is a white-tailed deer, *odocoileus virginianus*, the smallest and most nervous member of the North American deer family.

How many deer have I seen dead at the side of a road in my lifetime? Hundreds for sure, maybe a thousand. The top of the deer's head points toward the pavement where it died, the neck stretched long in the grass and the single visible eye brown, glassy, and wide, as if a taxidermist had set it there, placed it in a patient form ready for portraiture or mounting. Among all animals deer possess one of the most graceful figures, trim and defined, shapely and economical, finely tuned, vibrating with beauty. Fleet of foot, and short of life. I would like their portrait to be painted by Lucien Freud, bathed in bright light like his sleeping whippets, lying in an intimate mesh, without the shadow of death.

For days no one moved the dead deer. How many drivers passed by, saw the corpse, and kept going? A thousand? Two thousand? Thousands more drove by and noticed no carcass at the side of the road—so familiar and common as to be invisible, "an incident of roadside mortality," as the township's Deer Management Plan puts it. What about the residents in the condominiums—don't they mind looking out on a dead deer? Or are they skilled in not seeing it? They park their car in the allotted space and hurry inside, not noticing what lies in the grass about them.

To consider the dead deer, to dwell upon its prone body, is to risk being seen as sentimental. This infantile emotional overflow, this unexamined response, is well known to me. But I don't think my emotions are sentimental—that is, exaggerated and self-indulgent, shallow and uncomplicated. My neighbor feeds the deer to tempt them close, to ensure that she has pretty pictures outside her window. They're cute, she says, they're dear. *That* is sentimental. When I tell her that feeding wildlife can be detrimental, do more damage than good, she waves me off. At Christmastime reindeer lit with white lights are installed in her front yard.

Sighting, November 22. Before getting into bed, I open the sliding door a few inches to ventilate the room while we sleep. A loud rustle below our second-story bedroom. Snap on the outside floodlights. Hear more rustling and step out onto the balcony to see what it might be: two small deer frozen in the leaf-strewn ivy. Their faces turn toward me and they don't move, not one little bit, as if a single light holds them in place and time.

None of the common attitudes toward deer I'm aware of entirely fits me. I'm not an animal rights activist who is set against hunting in every instance, not a biologist, not a certified naturalist, not a hunter who eats what he kills and believes he has a primal relationship with deer, not a painter, not a member of the township's herd management team. Perhaps I am a metaphysician, alive to the beauty of the deer—but that's only part of my feelings. Once we moved to our house set in the trees near the Red Cedar River, deer became implicated in my life, and I've become implicated in theirs. We share a home range; their lives and deaths intersect with mine. This much we share, but their lives are pitiably short and hard, and this brute brevity has burrowed inside to trouble me. Home range can be a tricky concept, and its extent depends greatly on the quality of forage, protective cover, water, and other factors. The range for the deer in my area may be as small as a one-quarter square mile.

When we bought the house five years ago, we had no idea what lived among these trees, near this river, what would pass through our property. At first my response to the wildlife veered towards the joyful, pure, and simple. I was made happy by the blue heron staking out a fishing spot every afternoon on the bank across the river. Waking on one of our first mornings in the new house, I saw three deer under the crabapple eating the hard little fruit that had fallen. I sighed with pleasure. My impulse was not to fly out into the yard clapping and screaming, as my neighbors did, bent on stopping the devouring of one's garden. My visitors moved from crabapple to hostas, tearing off one leaf and then another until mere ragged stalks remained. I felt no ownership of the yard. They'd lift a watchful head, chomping, green leaves the size of a peony sticking out of a soft mouth.

My first autumn in the house I tried to offer apples to the deer as if they were horses, a misguided experiment in presumption. I wasn't so stupid as to hold the apple in my hand and expect them to come to me. I threw the apples in their direction, but of course I merely frightened them. They didn't know it was a harmless and edible meal hurling through the air towards them. Next I tried leaving apples in spots they passed through. The squirrels got them before the deer.

Sighting, November 23. Early morning. Ice on the roof. Light in the backyard. Two deer, mother and medium-sized fawn, look up at the house, where I stand still in the family room behind the full-length windows. They're nervous, constantly alert for movement, sound, threat—I've never seen a deer that wasn't nervous, except the exhausted and the dead. They look back and forth between the river and the house. The mother moves first and in front while the fawn scours the ground. Not much left this late in fall—the deer have been through this yard more times than I can know. The fawn sniffs the dry hydrangeas, just reedy stalks and brown flower heads. The mother is too busy observing to eat. She can't relax enough to bend her neck to the grass; she must stand with ears pricked and eyes darting, the white ring under her neck clear to see. Eventually they skitter through into my neighbor's yard and are gone. Only then do I move from the window.

Our house lies in what the Michigan Department of Resources calls an urban/suburban area: residential developments and businesses mixed with undeveloped wetlands that can't be built upon, parks and natural areas, and open fields from the area's farming past. This suburban environment has created what deer biologists call *edge*, that is, crop fields juxtaposed with meadow and woods, natural preserves, and enriched residential yards. Deer need food, water, and cover primarily. My subdivision, surrounding neighborhoods, and intermixed open lands form a high-quality habitat where they flourish. No one knows how many deer this home range supports; no exact count has been undertaken. The main threat to the population is the high-density traffic that flows on arteries like Hamilton Road.

When I turn off Hamilton to enter Tacoma Hills, the houses are spread far apart on big lots, the trees become large and dense. We have no sidewalks, curbs, or streetlights, and neighborhood covenants prohibit fences in front yards. The houses circle a lagoon, back up to three natural areas, and cluster around a large Commons between the two streets that intersect with Hamilton and are the only entrances to the subdivision. The Red Cedar

River forms the southern boundary. I can walk out my back door, launch my kayak, and in minutes no longer see houses.

My house is placed in a wood of big oaks and maples, with more settled landscaping front and back. The deer browse here throughout the year, although in winter they may simply pass through on the way to better forage. In the warmer months they lie in the fallen leaves at the edges of the yard. Last spring a tiny fawn, separated from its mother, spent a whole afternoon in the tall ferns under the redbud tree. It slept so soundly that I worried it had been abandoned. I brought a bowl of water and set it five feet away, but the fawn never drank. After a long walk that evening, I found it had departed. Perhaps the fawn had been hidden under the redbud while its mother looked for food and was reclaimed.

Sighting, December 9, 4:46 P.M. 26 degrees, light snow on the ground, blue sky splattered with large patches of delicate pink tinged with orange. In thirty minutes the sky will go dark. The deer arrive at this turning time. A herd of twelve is running on the other side of the river, scattered out across the snow, bounding in what looks like wild abandon. I watch them from the kitchen sink as I snap the beans for dinner. Sometimes deer walk through the yard or along the banks of the river in single file, with a purpose, looking down for food, then freeze, listening for threat. No such caution tonight—they are like children who have been cooped up all day inside a classroom and have been released into the schoolyard for recess.

How apt it is for the word *deer* to be both singular and plural. Nouns with identical singular and plural forms are often the names of animals: moose, sheep, bison, salmon, pike, trout, swine, elk, and shrimp. We seldom think of them as unique, as singular, as individuals. Like the carcass at the roadside on Hamilton, deer are always off to the side, standing at the margins. Rushing by, drivers don't ask whether they know *that* deer or not. We see them out of the corner of our eye if we see them at all. Only the hunter sees the deer dead center in his sights. I want to move the deer to the center of my picture.

Do I know the deer? *Know* is too strong a word, for it implies a human intimacy and familiarity, an explicit relationship that I can't claim. Still, deer come through my yard regularly, and this Hamilton deer may well have visited a hundred times, stood below my window while I slept, munched my hostas while I watched. When its eyes were alive, our eyes may have met. If know doesn't precisely describe the relationship, what word does? We co-habit this range, are residents of the land and also temporary dwellers. I do not know whether I figure in the deer's memory or imagination or whether thinking in those terms is plausible. The deer establish patterns, I occupy a spot on their range map, and in that sense they know my house and the lay of the land about it. Do they recognize me? I doubt it, not in the sense humans understand the concept. But it is possible they recognize me in a form of sense memory. Primarily deer look at me to determine whether I am a threat. Do they learn over time that I am not, or is their reaction to me only and ever as a possible threat? Certain groups that stand at hedges, around the yards, in the fields and natural areas, I register as *familiar*: "That's the doe and two fawns that came through yesterday," I say to myself. Right now a group is browsing at my neighbor's two doors down; a doe pauses below the back balcony, munching a hedge she'd disdain if it weren't barren winter. Now a fawn, and another, joins her in the hedge destruction. They drift over to my yard to check out the bird feeder. This isn't the trio that before my eyes hungrily raided it the previous week. The doe is wary of the feeder, checks it with her tongue, sniffs something she doesn't like, and backs away. When one of the fawns tries to take a turn, she swats it away with her head. They move on to the backyard and find vegetation to consume where I see nothing.

There is one particular deer I catch sight of all over the subdivision. (I think of it as the same deer, though I may be collapsing several individuals into one.) A young deer, a buck, underdeveloped, a little ungainly, a smallish head without antlers or poise, and alone, always a solitary traveler. When I spot it alone across the river, browsing or lying down, I think, "That is the deer I know." At the same time, I am in doubt, thinking I am imposing a familiarity upon these encounters.

When I see the animal at the side of Hamilton Road, I worry that it is the deer I know.

Sighting, later. Full moon when we walk with the dogs after dinner. Omar the retriever senses deer before I do, and his ears go up. A moment after, two deer dash through on our right and disappear behind a house. Omar wants to chase them. When I am in bed later, the full moon hangs visible through the skylights.

*Its light beams into my face and wakes me. I feel shot through
with cold light and called to the fields.*

In Middle English *der*, in Old English *deor*, meant a wild
animal of any kind, in contrast to cattle or other livestock that
could be pastured on designated land. Deer aren't domestic, like
a horse in a stable whose name is inscribed on the stall door, or
cows in a barn. They do not saunter over to the fence to see if
you have an apple. You cannot ride them for pleasure or compete
in a steeplechase. You cannot derive milk from them for butter
or cheese. You can't have a history with a deer in the usual sense.
They're wild, and no pasture contains them. They belong to no
one and come and go as they please.

December 11. Driving home on Mt. Hope, inappropriately
named given all the animal deaths that occur on it, I knew long
before I could see distinctly that a dead deer was lying on the
grassy shoulder, a border lightly dusted with snow. The deer's
head is facing the street, and blood has seeped from front and
back of its lithe body. Red dots of frozen blood in the snow. I
can't reconstruct what happened here. If the deer was crossing
from north to south, why wouldn't it be lying in the road; how
could the impact throw the body to land in this position? I am
probably the only person who wants to know how the deer
assumed its posture. No one thinks about how it happened or
why the deer assumes its final pose—not the way we are haunted
by people in the last throes of life. We have to know that the
heart attack came on suddenly as Uncle Harry was doing the
laundry and that's why he was found sprawled on the basement

floor with a black sock in his hand. What is it in me that needs to know about this animal? And suddenly I understand—it is natural to grab a carcass by the hind legs to pull it away from traffic.

It will be days before anyone removes the deer from the shoulder. I will see it many times on my way to and from work—I'll be looking for it, knowing it is there, unattended. I feel alone and cold, aware that the deer turns me around on myself, standing apart from other people.

Home, I start to make dinner. Out the back windows two deer lying down on the banks of the river. While chopping mushrooms and squash, I remember the survey the Meridian Township invited its residents to take in response to a plan to allow antlerless deer hunting on selected public, and perhaps private, lands. According to its website, the township had been receiving complaints from citizens saying, for example, "The deer are everywhere!" No statistics supported claims that the population had increased to an unhealthy, threatening number.[1] That, however, was the perception of the general populace. I knew it was pointless to fill out the survey, and that the township had already determined to allow managed hunts on parklands normally closed to hunting. Still, I answered the questions and

---

[1] The township's draft Deer Management Plan reads: "It is difficult to obtain exact numbers of the deer herd population." In other words, the township couldn't say with any convincing authority whether the number had indeed increased. Local biologists were quoted as saying that damage to vegetation and incidents of deer-vehicle accidents were sufficient measures to justify the hunts. I could find no statistics that would indicate a recent surge in deer-vehicle collisions.

voiced my concern about the lack of evidence in support of the conclusions reached. The survey asked for contact information, which I provided, so that I might be gotten back to. No one called, no one wrote.

Determining a good size for the deer population in a town like ours is not settled by figuring out how many deer the land can support. A decision also depends on what people feel about their interactions with deer. At one of the meetings of the Environmental Commission, an expert emphasized the need for democratic discussion to determine the township's stance on deer. Some residents—farmers, garden enthusiasts, and those who have experienced an automobile-deer collision—will prefer a low density, while others who have a higher tolerance for the problems deer cause will prefer a higher density. On the spectrum of possible values, I place myself on the high end of tolerance. Yet I am concerned with the quality of life and the health of the deer. If overpopulation can be demonstrated, along with the deterioration of health and habitat, I would favor a management plan. [2]

At a dinner party where the township's managed hunts were discussed, one of the women called deer "giant rats with antlers" and was pleased that their numbers would be thinned. She and her husband maintain a substantial garden and an orchard, and deer are the enemy. They occupy a place on the low end of deer

---

[2] In all the materials deer are treated as a resource that government agencies have a right to manage. And manage they have—decreasing or increasing their number as the historical moment dictates

tolerance. Her relish at their demise reminded me of a hunter neighbor who each year hangs his latest trophy from a jungle gym to drain the blood before dressing. He has a fenced backyard that would shield the carcass from his neighbors' view, but that would not display his achievement. Residents have asked him to move the deer, which disturbed their children, but he refuses. At the dinner party I felt troubled in a way that has been familiar to me since childhood. Conversation about subjects I care deeply about at a dinner party will not allow me to express myself in a way that feels true or even okay. When I've been unguarded enough to say something real, the emotions blast out and spray everyone around me in the face and it isn't pleasant for anyone. When it comes to my views about animals, I always feel at the margin. It was a group of educated companions who felt certain of their priority over animals. Not troubled, not questioning, not pausing, not a disturbed stirring arose that suggested the matter of harvesting deer was complicated. There was no place for feelings, or feelings of the sort I am burdened by. After my frustration with them and with myself built up sufficient pressure, I blurted out, "I prefer deer to human beings." I don't know if that is true, but I said it because I was enflamed, compelled to throw a hand grenade into the dinner chat. Afterward I felt embarrassed and exposed. I wanted to leap over a fence and disappear. You might expect that my daffy outburst offended my companions. It did not. They didn't take me seriously.

December 12. Dead deer still there at the side of Mt. Hope.

Sighting, late night. In the dark I let my dogs out into the side yard. On automatic pilot, sleepy, I do not think about the wildlife they might surprise. When I turn on the back lights, I see a shape at the bottom of the yard. The dogs don't immediately see or sense the solitary deer, much larger than usual. It moves slightly up from the river and Omar sees it. He charges toward it but halfway to his goal stops. This deer stood his ground. When Omar came back, he bounds up the porch steps and back into the house.

December 13. Deer gone; removed.

Sighting, December 19, midmorning. Four deer, a doe and three semi-grown fawns, in the yard. In the daylight the deer often stay down by the river. The winter hunger is changing the behavior of this group—they're awfully close. Between browsings, the mother licks the fawns, head and neck, and then moving down the back. The fawns lick her, too, and they touch heads and rub necks.

Midafternoon we drive on Dobie Road to our friends' house to drop off Christmas cookies. On the way home an hour later, I see a dead deer at the side of the road that wasn't there on the outbound trip. I wonder if I know this deer.

December 20, morning. I go out of my way to see if the deer is still on Dobie. I can't see it driving south. But when I turn around and return going north, I spot it. It has fallen a good way off the road and is shielded by brush and shrubs. "Still there," I say out loud. Still there. What is wrong with me?

December 20, noon. I take my camera and walk with the dogs across Sander Farm. We pass the deep red barn on which figures painted in white announce the settling of the land in 1875. This barn and another a little farther north are remnants of the rural past, when the area was predominantly fields of crops. Stoplights have been installed along Dobie at several spots, but it's a terrible trap for deer—two narrow lanes, with a speed limit pegged to its semirural nature; if you swerve, you'll run into oncoming traffic or fly up on the sidewalk. But deer cross the road in numbers, coming and going from the Dobie Reserve, an undeveloped swathe of land that the Red Cedar River runs through. My deer was on its way to the fence that borders the Reserve, or had just surmounted it. Less than a hundred yards away is a stoplight, and fifty yards away a bus stop.

Last summer a small deer died in the Commons. A member of the neighborhood association board of trustees called the Ingham County Roads Commission, which informed him that the ICRC only picks up carcasses from public roads. So a neighbor tilted the animal onto a tarp and dragged it out to the street. In two days it vanished. It was through this incident that I learned who removes deer from roads.

When I arrive home, I call the Road Commission about the deer on Dobie. The man I speak to says he'll fill out a work order to pick up the carcass since it is on a public road.

"What do you do with the deer once you pick it up?" I ask.

"Relocate it," he says, to a place where it can decompose naturally and won't bother anyone.

If the deer is already too far gone to be moved, the Road Commission douses it with lime.

December 22. Something is building in me—I can't get deer out of my head or eyes. Wherever I look, I see deer. And I don't look away. I don't say I have something better to do. Out my study window in the side yard or at the bird feeder, in the back, down by the river, lying down, at night when I let the dogs out, there they are, in the morning under my window, walking in Sander Farm, dead on all the roads I drive to get to work, to go anywhere. I'm trying to sort it, as the British, say. *Sort it* covers a multitude of meanings—figure out what's going on, what you feel, fix it—it being some form of trouble, of confusion, of malfunction. But in this case, I don't think anything is malfunctioning. All my senses and feelings seem in high alert, watchful, fully alive and engaged. Something inside me says, "Look, here they come, the deer, pay attention. This is a moment in time like no other, when what is ordinary becomes something else."

Sighting, December 28. Deer across the river, lying down. I get out my binoculars and count them: seven. Bright sun, blue skies, and biting cold. They're scattered, not far from each other. Hours go by in this resting position. At 4:30 one deer gets up, and then another, and eventually all seven are on their feet. Not doing much. Cleaning, urinating, more cleaning, taking slow, leisurely steps down to the river, drinking. Calm. Then my husband lets our dogs out into the side yard before he feeds them. The dogs are on the other side of the river from the deer, a long way away. Each deer freezes and look across the river at the dogs. At first none of them looks alarmed—they're just paying attention. And then, as if in response to something I can't detect, all seven lift their white tails and bound in a group out of the woods.

With deer, we cannot know and we cannot be known in the usual sense—there's a freedom in that, freedom from the usual forms of feeling. The deer emerge out of the woods and take me away with them. I put down my task, look out, and suddenly the window becomes enormous and I feel shaken awake. Maybe the deer reintroduce me to parts of myself I thought I had lost or thwarted—a capacity for receiving a vibration of beauty that has rearranged the wiring of my brain.

Sighting, January 1. Off Dobie Road, on my way to a trailhead, a bit of undeveloped land. Getting out of my car, I glimpse in the corner of my eye a young buck on the other side of the railroad tracks that parallel the trail. I walk toward the opening of light made by the right of way. At first he doesn't sense my presence. When he picks me out of the landscape, he rotates his head and focuses, like a camera adjusting a zoom lens. I expect him to disappear into the trees, for that's what deer do, flee, lifting tails high in white dismissal. But when this creature moves, he moves toward me. I try to hold my ground, but unwittingly I shift. And at that, the deer turns and leaps into the brush.

I keep after him, following his course. I spot him again, atop a mound of colorful cardboard boxes and other garbage, on the track behind him an abandoned railroad car, red and black with graffiti. His eyes hang on an invisible line running to me. We share a moment. And then with a snort that hangs in the air, long, humid, and velvet-lined, he jumps for the woods and disappears.

If I could I would follow him anywhere.

January 3. News reports say that residents of Meridian Township have responded positively to the managed hunts. Among respondents to the survey, 72.7 percent answered yes to this question: "Have you or a member of your family experienced or come close to a deer/vehicle accident in Meridian Township?" The question provides no time frame—in the last year, in the last ten years? What does "come close to" mean? It is impossible to ascertain from the results whether there has been a real increase in collisions, or a perceived one. A managed hunt was approved by 74.6 percent of respondents, 68.9 percent favored "encouragement of residents to hunt or allow hunting on large parcels of private property, defined as five acres or more." As of today, forty-one deer have been harvested, and the township board has approved an extension of the hunt through the end of February.

MY FATHER'S SHOES

The day my father died we drove in the bright, tilted light of autumn, past farms, pastures, and ponds, finally arriving at the orchard. We parked the car, picked up two half-bushel bags to fill, and walked up Orchard Lane, the trail of powdered dust, fine as confectioner's sugar, that led to the grove. That's when I noticed them—my father's shoes on my husband's feet.

They're old man's shoes, beige like the walls in retirement homes that take in widows and widowers when they have nowhere else to go. That's where my father moved after my mother died, where by each identical door, on a little ledge, the resident displayed plastic flowers and stuffed animals.

I was disconcerted when Richard wore his shoes. I didn't want him to put his feet where my father's feet had rested. On the trail up the hill, Richard was shuffling like my father did the last time I saw him.

When we entered the lane of Mutsu trees under clear blue skies with fast moving clouds and the grass growing tall between the trees, the light went very pale. I no longer knew exactly who I was: was I a daughter following the footsteps of my father or a wife following my husband? Was my father dead or resurrected in my husband? Richard moved down the lane and disappeared inside the canopy of a tree. I could only see his shoes, my father's shoes, glistening in the wet grass.

DEER/CONFIDENTIAL

This is the landscape of obsession.

Spring (1)

The doe outside my study window is lame. Sometimes she is alone. Sometimes she has two fawns with her and sometimes she has three.

The fawns are tiny and they don't know what to do without her.

Last night two fawns came running to her with tails wagging. They made little sounds and started nursing while their tails wagged. I don't know if that is the proper word to describe what the tails of deer do when they are happy. After a few minutes of their exuberance, she pushed them away and moved off.

I worry about them all the time. She is off-balance, teetering, on the verge of collapse. She has three fawns attached to her.

Fall (1)

Deer hunt. In Meridian Township where I live the powers that be have expanded their deer culling—from October to February. Adding several months. Now I must watch passively while the deer I know are killed. The three fawns and their limping mother may not will surely not (say it!) make it. This above all else opens a world of suffering for me, to underlie everything.

I've been perched on the edge of the river that does not move and perhaps will never move and now the cord keeping me is thin and ready to break. I've started my leave-taking.

Embracing, fully, my loner status. If it comes with a certain melancholy, so be it.

The hunters are in tree stands, shooting down.

I can't detach

from the deer. They come into the yard. I don't own this land. I just carry a mortgage and a deed. They come from the Berry's yard, past my study windows and then hang out looking for food, accepting certain plants, rejecting others, hungrily. They smell things. They listen, ever vigilant. And then they pass through.

~~I can think of nothing but deer.~~

Perhaps because my mother is dead, I am writing about deer. Deer have become my flood subject. This does not bode well for my career. My mother is a venerable subject, a Lady Macbeth. The mother is a venerable subject. Though some editors say they're done with mothers as if anyone could ever be finished with mother. My mother lives in my spine. Deer are invisible to most people ~~but not me, never me~~—we've learned to not see them at the side of the road ~~but not me, never me~~ as we're racing to wherever we must go. Deer are plentiful so why should we perturb ourselves when they die? How to write about this subject and transcend its difficulties? Too ordinary, too sentimental, the poor battered body. ~~Too close.~~

I don't fill up my days with talk, I don't lie well or flatter, I am aloof and hard to please, I am wary. I am ~~probably~~ a minor writer; ~~I am a deer,~~ a minor animal.

Why aren't people strangled by doubt? ~~I am.~~

~~In almost all ways I feel the need to start over.~~

Dream: a woman who cut my hair many years ago, emerges from behind a door in a room I am seated in. She sits down behind me in a swivel chair. I am seated in a hard-backed chair like the kind from elementary school. She can't stand. Her brain tumors and the treatments she underwent have left her off-balance, ~~weak.~~ Her hand holding the scissors shakes. She can't cut straight. But then she isn't so much cutting my hair as she's weaving it into corkscrew ropes that she twists to stand out from my head like

Medusa's snakes. Is this what she thinks I need now in my life—
hair that repels?

Winter (1)

The deer on Mt. Hope, on the right side, near the black fence,
farther down from the cemetery. Who knows where in the road
the car hit the deer. What I know is that the deer was hit with
enough force to throw her up onto the curb, twisted in the way
only hit deer twist, contorted, her neck turned to face oncoming
traffic, eyes still open, the face delicate and lovely, the body in an
upheaval, with the back legs elevated into the air and almost at
cross-purposes.

Expert in what will not bloom, what will not move, stilled by a
force of unmaking, a footnote at the hem of winter's white dress,
barely seen.

She has been there for days. No one has moved her even though
she lies on a public road. No one has called.

Now with last night's storm, she is buried under snow. Just the
rear hooves can be seen peeking out of the snow.

I worry she is ~~my~~ the lame deer. Impossible to believe that she
could make it through this unrelenting winter with non-stop
snow. Impossible to jump fences or move through the fields so
deep in snow.

Found what I think is the remainder of a deer near the fence by the river at the end of the street. Something has dug it clear of snow. Blood smears.

I cannot sleep.

Deer. ~~The deer is a vision of my own vulnerability.~~ I fear for the deer, especially the lame or the small, I fear for what awaits, what they must navigate. When I see one dead, I am shaken, I feel as if a little more of me is dying each time, ~~that I am becoming more and more vulnerable.~~

Abandoned at the side of the road—not even a death deep in the woods or pasture. Disposable. ~~Vulnerable and disposable is what I feel or fear, that everything I have tried to do with my one life is pointless, amounts to nothing, goes unrecognized, will disappear in a flash.~~ The deer means that to me. It wasn't so when I was younger. Then it was the horse. It was the horse I held in my chest under my left breast.

Dream: Walking up the stones to a friend's house, little glass bottles filled with flowers and cards tied at the neck. Don't know what the cards say just that there are cards. A birthday party? Then downstairs, her son falls head first into a hole and I haul him out and wash him off and he hangs around my neck and stays there. I feel wonderful holding him. ~~But I fear he is not long for this world. Is a ghost.~~

On the score of my own writing, I have accomplished little ~~nothing~~. Failure everywhere I look.

I know something about a throttle by the throat, a force like hands about me.

I know something about the absence of movement—the river gutted for a lifetime of todays.

Late Winter/Early spring

Saw a deer late this morning on the ice of the river, stuck. The ragged-tailed squirrels dangled like beggars in glossy branches so brittle they stung. The ice is thawing and the river is terribly wide. Somehow this deer managed to get there and not know how to get off the river. Slippery —the ice made slippery because it was raining, melting the snow that gave it traction. At last the deer leapt onto our banks, didn't make it, fell into the water, and then with the greatest of difficulty managed to scramble up the bank. I feared it would hurt its legs ~~fatally~~. He made it, then stood and shook the water from his coat and shivered.

~~I wait with hope in my throat.~~

Earlier still this morning I thought I saw my lame doe crossing through our yard on the way to the corn my neighbors have spread in their back yard. She was with her usual three others. It

was her. ~~No doubt.~~ Same dangling leg and slow gait. ~~How I care.~~
~~It matters to me.~~

Troubling:

1. I am helpless before all the big important things in life.
2. I need to say this again—I am helpless.
3. I am a loner. My voice is small. ~~No one hears me. Nothing will change that.~~
4. Did I do something to create this solitary stance?
5. I can unplug the drain, wash the dirt from the floors, close the windows if I don't want rain to come in, but I can't stop plunder, and I can't keep the deer safe.

Fall Again

"With a growing deer population, the Meridian township is trying to expand its deer management program. Hunters have been allowed on certain public properties. Now the township wants to expand that to private land."

The deer become more frantic, less predictable. ~~I become more frantic.~~ A whole group of deer running through the yard at the border of the river, large dark bodies plunging through.

An odd buck trailing behind a group. His head is covered in grey gauze that falls to his chest. The other deer don't trust him and run from him when he approaches. Just like everyone else, the deer shy away from what is different. They shun him.

Saw him the next morning on the river—he was following them and they were running away.

Two deer walking, one behind the other; the one in the rear resting his head on his mother's rump.

The deer with the gauzy headdress is in the river. I walk down to the fire circle to try to see what's on his head. He turns away from me, stands facing a tree. His aloneness is burdensome, sorrowful. ~~Burdensome, sorrowful.~~

Someday I will be done with being vetted, evaluated, accepted, rejected. It can't come too soon.

Deer found in the lagoon. Dead. It was the buck with the gauzy headdress. A lawn ornament stuck on his antlers that he couldn't get off.

An eleven-year-old boy killed an albino buck. A rarity. Thirty yards away he was, with a bow and arrow. Photo shows the beautiful albino buck and the boy, common as dirt.

Forty-five deer have been harvested with seventy-two volunteer hunters on twenty-two properties within the township.

Two hundred and fifty deer have been harvested in managed hunts over the last three years.

The hunters are in tree stands, shooting down.

Two deer walking, one behind the other; the one in the rear resting his head on his mother's rump.

The deer I know are here and they are thin. Especially the mother. In the beginning, they were toy deer, petite and spotted. Now in late October they have lost their spots and are filling out and taller. Today there are only two fawns and I wonder, as I always do, what has happened to the third.

The hunters are in tree stands, shooting down.

Miraculous that the limping doe is still alive. Looks like she was hit by a car. Yesterday she collapsed in a pile of leaves at the bottom of the yard by the river.

But here she is.

I don't know why I follow her. She is in pain, yet she is on the move all day. She anchors these fawns. Who do I anchor? I am not lame. I am not hungry. I am not hunted. Am I?

The stars have aligned that she should choose my yard.

I think about how she will die and it shatters me.

The hunters are in tree stands, shooting down.

I come home from work to find my doe lying in the leaves. Chewing. Looking at me.

Late Winter, Again

I can't let go. I have lists of all the things I can't let go of. They fill a small notebook.

Yesterday was a terrible day. A cold front moved in. Driving on Mt. Hope, there she was—another dead deer hit by a car and flipped up onto the curb in the spot where all the deer die on the right side of the road by the gates of the cemetery. This one was winter dark and thin.

I think ~~for the thousandth time~~ it is my doe. She has met her end. After making it through the hardest winter in decades, she's hit by a car crossing Mt. Hope. An end long foretold. Will I stop worrying about her now? Or does my worry outlive her?

If I don't call for her removal, she'll rot. I will watch the process of her disintegration.

I will call. How many deer have I personally had removed from Mt. Hope? Too many.

Omen for the day ahead, a day filled with a kind of professional dying. No one threatened my health. No one battered me with their car or ran at me with a sword, no one aimed their arrow or their gun upon me. But there are many ways to die.

There are no vibrations of beauty in the air I breathe.

Have you ever come close to death?
I listen more than I speak.

I don't know if deer hear anything besides the sounds of what might hurt them—a car approaching, dogs on the run, a hunter's boots crunching in the leaves.

We regret to inform you.

I don't think my doe is alive. I haven't seen her for some time.

I've been trying, unsuccessfully to not feel so much. I feel too much. It's a problem. I am advised to turn away.

She and I are one. I feel certain she is dead. The last time I saw her come through her leg was swollen, two or three times the size it had been. I felt the chill. Her crew still makes their circuit but she is gone. I mistakenly thought I was going forward. It was a dream. ~~I am on a downward slope, sliding away, and there's a kind of death taking place, the death of chances.~~

The shadow of death is coming. I feel it in the morning, in the middle of the night when I wake up. In bed. I think about lying down underneath a tree on the edge of a path, looking up to the sky.

I need to remember I am nothing.
I am nothing and nothing comes to nothing.

The river is melting.

There is a plan afoot to cull the deer in Dobie Preserve, the natural area right down the street from me which I walk every day. It is a deer sanctuary. I suspect that the eleven or twelve deer I see coming through my yard are the herd from which they will cull. They lie under my trees in the leaves and look at me.

The hunters are in tree stands, shooting down.

Spring Again

Sunrise & fog. Rain last night. The sky a faint milky blue, the trees stark and grey, leaves on the banks of the river from last fall, wet and brown. Windless. The river, full from the snow melt, is not churning or rushing, but looks still, even though it isn't. The river is never still, it's always moving, but from the house, it looks still and a thick murky brown with a white mist rising above it. Five deer the color of the trees and the leaves and the river, their coats still a winter dark, stand on the banks of this side of the river looking to the other side. There always appears to be an impulse, a call, if you will, to get to the other side. There are always two sides, one bright and one dark, to the river. Here they are on the dark side but they don't want to stay. They want to cross over to where forsythia sings in a green grass. And eventually they do, one by one. The first deer sags down the bank alone, eases almost imperceptibly into the river and begins to swim across, blending into the river water. Only the deer's head bobs above the water's rim, all the other motions are quiet and don't ruffle the stillness. After the first deer reaches the other side and scampers up the bank and then runs into the trees shaking off the river with a flourish of leaps do the other four deer enter the river and swim in a group across, the same sleek movements, only the heads steering forward. By the time they are all assembled on the other side weaving in and out of the trees, the sun has fully risen, the blue become less milky, still a weak blue but blue nonetheless, and the light hitting the flanks of the deer illuminate them. Instead of the roughed up dark fur of just a half hour ago, they almost glitter.

THE UNDOING
(THE GREAT MICHIGAN ICE STORM)

12/21, 10:42 p.m.: the power goes out—
Comes on, goes out, comes on,
Goes out for good.

We wait.

Freezing rain pelts the skylights above us, holes to the night sky, no moon. Trees along the river creak and groan, black branches twisted in ice, hiss and split, undoing themselves all through the night. 500 pounds per quarter inch of ice for this glaze event, this silver thaw. The weight breaks whole trees, snaps them like tinder. Sometimes one bad thing happens after another, everything I touch and everything that touches me is a poison, a toxic thistle no one should brush up against much less eat, an invasive species that can't be stopped. I want to pull this bad spell out at the root, yank it to kingdom come but there is no *at the root*; the tendrils of misfortune, spiny and studded and tenacious, have spread underground all the way to the river and neither fire nor flood nor ice can destroy them.

12/22, 7:59 a.m.: with trackers strapped to our boots, we walk the iced-over ground, find post-apocalyptic trees ripped open, *gaping*, split down the middle the way my mother's hair turned grey in one streak of lightening after her husband died, caught in a collapsed steel mine. A million little matchsticks are strewn across the frozen wastes, dogwoods and serviceberries bowed down and sunk into the snow. There's something about not being able to do a thing that makes me let go, step out of myself, give over and give up the idea that I control anything. I am at the mercy of the storm; I am not entitled to a happy life, to food or warmth or berries at my feet. I can make nothing happen. I am but an honored guest at the ice buffet.

> Begin descent
> from the plateau of yard
> down the canal of railway ties
> cut into the snow-crusted hill;
> slide unceremoniously
> in an epic push
> to stand on the frozen river,
> a new birth story;
>
> See the gap between
> the river's ice
> and
> exposed tree roots—
> a thaw zone

A rusty drain pipe
2 feet in width
down the side of a yard
hangs over the river's edge
a frozen waterfall
stillbirth in its mouth;
uprooted trees sprung free
sprawl across ice:
abandoned vessels.

One winter when I was seven, skating on the river below our house with kids from the neighborhood, Mike's dog Rusty fell into a hole, a thaw zone, near the stone bridge. I fell in after him, the ice splintering all around me as I tried to pull us out. The hole got bigger and bigger until no one could reach us and the kids receded to the banks.

We see no one on the river—it is as if we are the last people alive, the last couple. No one ventures out to survey the damage, to clear the glass trees lit through with sunlight, to see the spun, blown glass arching over the river. The field's maize-colored grasses, heavy with ice, kneel over—whole fields of them bowed in submission. We walk on the river, not the land. Why do I feel melancholy walking in the middle of the Red Cedar River? Has my mood been created by my memory or has the river created it? I remember what it was like to swim under the ice, to be unable to touch bottom, to wait for rescue.

Too cold, the footing too treacherous. Not even the squirrels are out and the deer are bedded together deep wherever deer go in a storm front. They aren't ready to venture out yet. Not more than a week ago, when I was washing dishes, I looked up from the sink and saw a herd of deer across the river in the snow-filled woods. They were running in wide circles, looping round and round the horizon. No one was chasing them, but the chase was in their blood.

There, the concrete remains of an abandoned bridge: a face to be written on.

Under the new bridge on Dobie Road, a carcass of a deer. Recently enough killed that the blood still mixes in the snow and ice: mess of fur, bare leg bones, and a fleshless rib cage. No stink in this cold. Was it hit by a car, did it limp to the river to die or did it fall through the ice and drown? The coyotes found it— the coyotes whose existence some people dispute here in mid-Michigan—but I've seen at least one coyote running on the edge of the bank by the river, an outlier. Sometimes the deer want to cross from one side of the river to the other. Last winter one stood at the edge of our yard for the longest time looking out at the river. She wanted to cross—I could feel it. I wanted to cross over too. She was wondering if the river was frozen enough to support her. The snow had formed a bed over the ice, making it hard to tell how thick the ice was. If she ventured across she would fall in and then I would fall in too.

12/22, 5:03 p.m.: darkness falls. House lit with candles. Standing at the sink in the faintly-lit dark, I feel something outside my windows in the backyard. Sometimes before seeing I feel a change in vibrations, a rearrangement of the atoms in the air. I walk outside to the balcony and below me a large herd of deer, come out of hiding at the end of the day, gather and look up at me in a strange kind of healing on this winter night. A motley crew, scruffy and winter-dark—the edges of their separate bodies disintegrate, undone by the night. Waiting for a sign that the storm is over, that the creaking and groaning and splitting will cease, they look to me as if I am their patron saint.

ACKNOWLEDGMENTS

Material has been adapted from the following publications:

"A Chair Inhabits a Dream," *Bellingham Review*
"Edge," *Animal*
"My Father's Shoes," *River Teeth*
"Deer/Confidential," *Hotel Amerika*
"The Undoing," *Madcap Review*

MARCIA ALDRICH is the author of the free memoir *Girl Rearing*, published by W.W. Norton, and of *Companion to an Untold Story*, which won the AWP Award in Creative Nonfiction. She is the editor of *Waveform: Twenty-First-Century Essays by Women*, published by the University of Georgia Press.

❀

COLOPHON

Text is set in a digital version of Jenson, designed by Robert Slimbach in 1996, and based on the work of punchcutter, printer, and publisher Nicolas Jenson. The titles here are in Futura.

✳

NEW MICHIGAN PRESS, based in Tucson, Arizona, prints poetry and prose chapbooks, especially work that transcends traditional genre. Together with DIAGRAM, NMP sponsors a yearly chapbook competition.

DIAGRAM, a journal of text, art, and schematic, is published bimonthly at THEDIAGRAM.COM. Periodic print anthologies are available from the New Michigan Press at NEWMICHIGANPRESS.COM.